T0118930

HAPPY Heart
and the circulatory system

JOURNEY THROUGH the
Human BODY

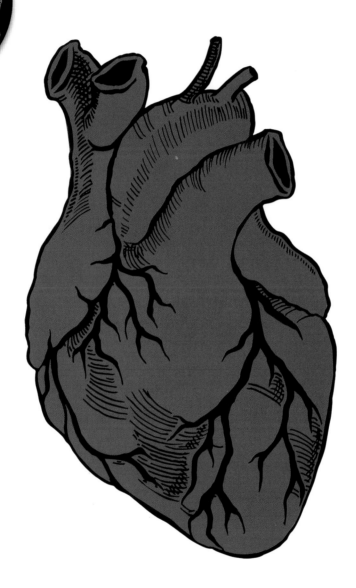

By
Charlie Ogden
Designed by Danielle Jones

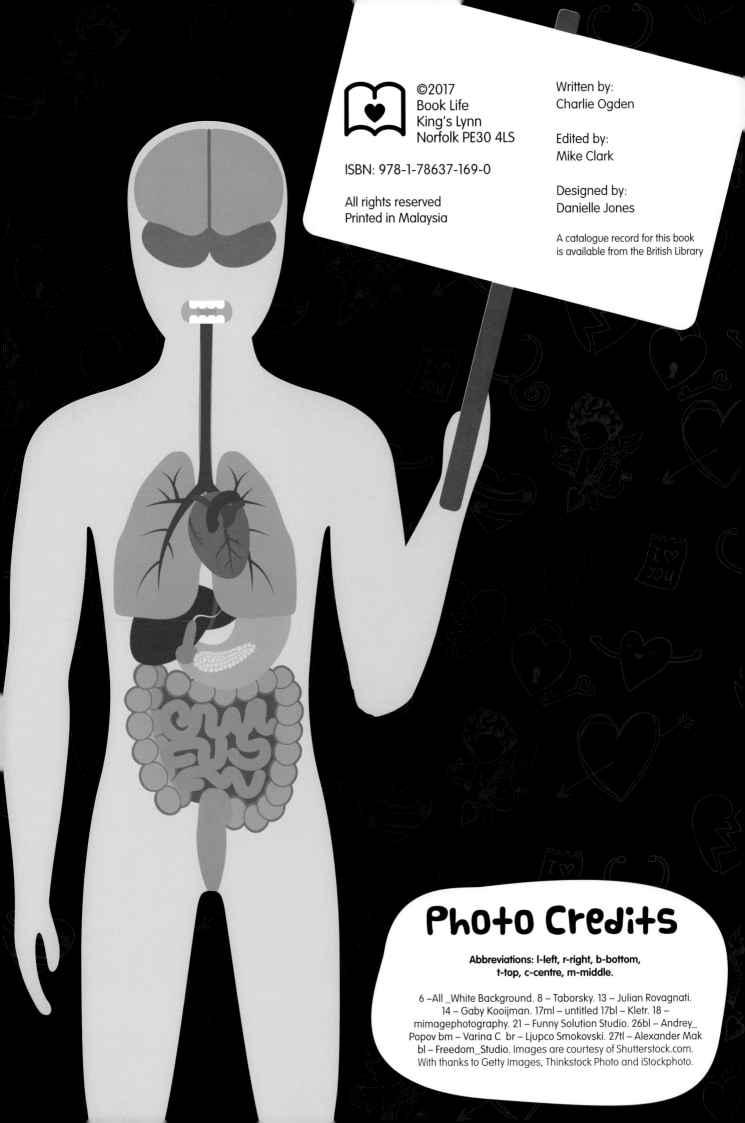

©2017
Book Life
King's Lynn
Norfolk PE30 4LS

ISBN: 978-1-78637-169-0

Written by:
Charlie Ogden

Edited by:
Mike Clark

Designed by:
Danielle Jones

All rights reserved
Printed in Malaysia

A catalogue record for this book
is available from the British Library

Photo Credits

Abbreviations: l-left, r-right, b-bottom,
t-top, c-centre, m-middle.

6 –All _White Background. 8 – Taborsky. 13 – Julian Rovagnati.
14 – Gaby Kooijman. 17ml – untitled 17bl – Kletr. 18 –
mimagephotography. 21 – Funny Solution Studio. 26bl – Andrey_
Popov bm – Varina C br – Ljupco Smokovski. 27tl – Alexander Mak
bl – Freedom_Studio. Images are courtesy of Shutterstock.com.
With thanks to Getty Images, Thinkstock Photo and iStockphoto.

HAPPY Heart

and the circulatory system

CONTENTS

Words that look like **this** are explained in the glossary on page 31.

Hi, I'm Dr. Anne Yurism. Follow me to start your journey through the circulatory system!

The HUMAN BODY

The human body is very complicated. The body is full of **organs**, bones, **muscles** and blood and all of these parts are wrapped up in a thin layer of skin. Because of this, finding your way around the human body can be very difficult and dangerous if you don't have a guide.

But lucky for you, I am here – so let our journey begin!

There are over **75 ORGANS** in the **HUMAN BODY!**

Systems of the Body

The first thing that you need to know about the body is that it uses **systems**. The systems of the body are made up of groups of organs that work together. Each system of the body has its own important job to do, such as stopping the body from getting sick or helping to keep the body strong.

There are lots of different systems in the body, but some are more important than others. Four of the most important systems in the body are:

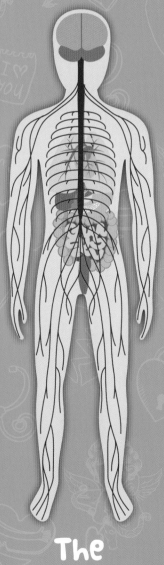

The Nervous System

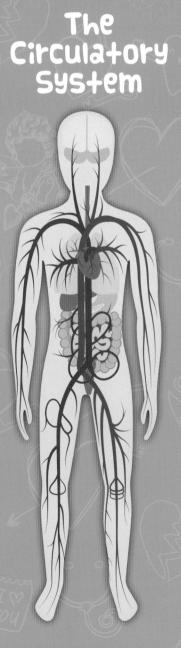

The Circulatory System

The Digestive System

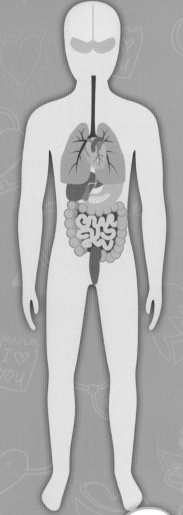

The Respiratory System

The CIRCULATORY SYSTEM

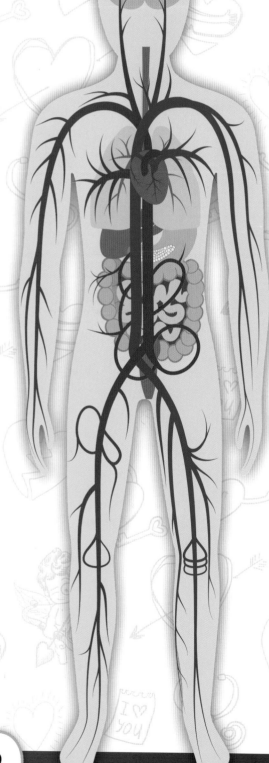

The circulatory system is made up of the heart and blood vessels. Blood vessels are tubes in the body that are made of **tissue**. These blood vessels stretch to every single part of the body, including the lungs and the brain.

The job of the circulatory system is to move blood around the body. The heart is an organ in the circulatory system that is made out of very strong muscles. The muscles in the heart can squeeze together to pump blood to every part of the body.

It is the circulatory system's job to move blood all around the body. Everyday, about five litres of blood are rushing around your body through your circulatory system.

What makes the circulatory system so important is that blood carries oxygen. Oxygen is a **gas** that is found in the air and all of the organs and muscles in the human body need oxygen to work properly. Blood vessels stretch to every part of the body because every part of the body needs the oxygen that is carried in the blood.

It only takes about **ONE MINUTE** for **BLOOD** to travel **ALL THE WAY THROUGH** the **CIRCULATORY SYSTEM.**

VESSEL Mania

If you laid out all of the **BLOOD VESSELS** in the human body in a line, it would **REACH AROUND THE EARTH TWO AND A HALF TIMES.**

There are three types of blood vessel in the body. They are:

ARTERIES

These blood vessels always carry blood away from the heart, usually towards the rest of the body. The blood carried in arteries usually has oxygen in it, as the blood hasn't yet reached the parts of the body that need the oxygen. When blood has oxygen in it, we say that the blood is oxygenated.

CAPILLARIES

After the blood has been pumped through the arteries, it goes into the capillaries. Capillaries are very tiny blood vessels inside the body's organs and muscles. The arteries take blood to the organs and muscles, but the capillaries take the blood through the organs and muscles. The capillaries make it so that the organs and muscles in the body can use the oxygen in the blood.

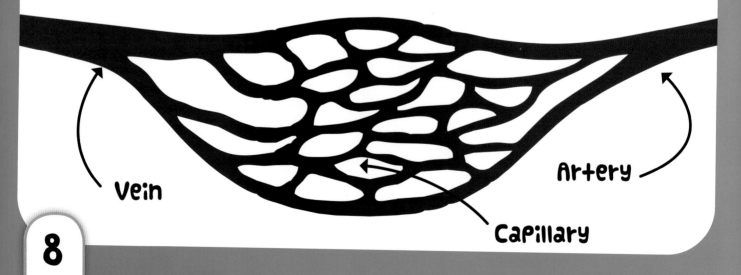

Vein

Artery

Capillary

VEINS

After the blood has gone through the capillaries, it goes into the veins. The blood that moves through veins is always going back towards the heart and it usually does not have oxygen in it. We call this deoxygenated blood. The oxygen in the blood was used up by the body when the blood moved through the capillaries.

An easy way to remember that **a**rteries take blood **a**way from the heart is by remembering that 'artery' and 'away' both begin with the letter **A**! Veins, on the other hand, always bring blood back towards the heart.

When we look at the blood vessels in our arms and legs, they look blue. This is not because the blood is blue. Blood vessels just appear blue when they are looked at through skin.

Look out for these signs. The pink section shows you where we are in the body!

Happy HEART

Next we move on to the best part of the circulatory system – the heart! The heart is the most important part of the circulatory system. It is made from very strong muscles and it is **hollow**.

The human heart takes in blood from a lot of different veins. When the heart is full of blood, it squeezes itself together. The heart is entirely made of muscle, meaning that it can squeeze itself together very tightly. When the heart squeezes itself together, it pushes blood into the arteries. This is what doctors mean when we say that the heart 'pumps' blood.

A child's heart is usually about the same size as their fist.

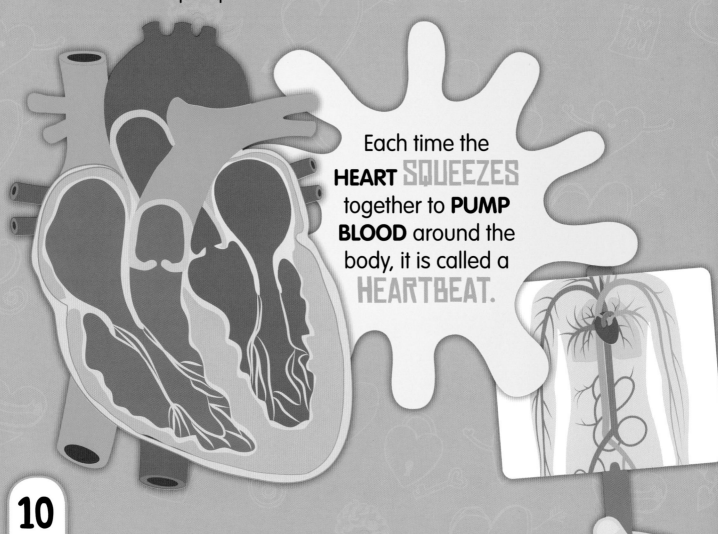

Each time the **HEART SQUEEZES** together to **PUMP BLOOD** around the body, it is called a **HEARTBEAT.**

TWO HALVES MAKE A WHOLE

The circulatory system is split into two parts. The first part of the circulatory system takes oxygenated blood around the body. Once the body has used the oxygen, the blood gets taken back to the heart. However, the blood that goes back to the heart from the body no longer has any oxygen in it.

This first part of the circulatory system is known as systemic circulation.

The second part of the circulatory system puts oxygen back into the blood. The heart also pumps deoxygenated blood to the lungs. Here, the blood can pick up more oxygen. It then gets pumped back to the heart so that it can take the oxygen around the body.

This second part of the circulatory system is known as pulmonary circulation.

Lungs

Blood from the lungs

OXGENATED

Blood to the lungs

DEOXGENATED

Heart

Blood to the body

Blood from the body

Body

O²

PUMP it UP

The heart is the most important part of the circulatory system because it pumps the blood around the body. Because there are two main parts to the circulatory system, there are also two main parts to the heart.

The right side of the heart takes in blood that has just been pumped around the body. This blood is deoxygenated, so the right side of the heart pumps it to the lungs so that it can pick up oxygen.

After the blood has picked up oxygen in the lungs, it is pumped back into the heart. This time, however, the blood is pumped into the left side of the heart. This side of the heart then pumps the oxygenated blood around the rest of the body.

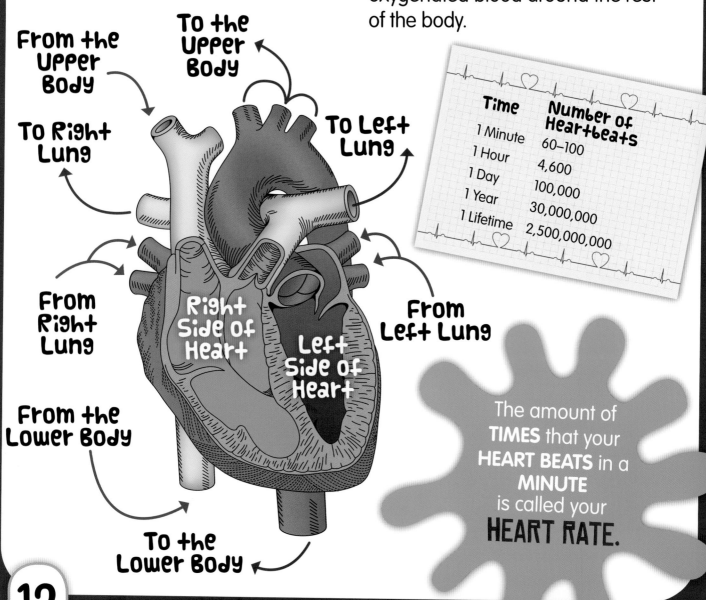

From the Upper Body

To the Upper Body

To Right Lung

To Left Lung

From Right Lung

From Left Lung

Right Side of Heart

Left Side of Heart

From the Lower Body

To the Lower Body

Time	Number of Heartbeats
1 Minute	60–100
1 Hour	4,600
1 Day	100,000
1 Year	30,000,000
1 Lifetime	2,500,000,000

The amount of **TIMES** that your **HEART BEATS** in a **MINUTE** is called your **HEART RATE.**

BLOOD-A-DUB-DUB

Sometimes the heart beats very quickly and other times the heart beats much slower. This is because the body doesn't always need the same amount of oxygen. The heart beats faster when the body needs more oxygen and more slowly when the body needs less oxygen.

You can feel your own **HEARTBEAT** in your **CHEST, NECK** and **WRIST**. Check your heart rate by counting how many times your heart beats in **60 SECONDS.**

The body needs more oxygen than usual when a person does **exercise**. This is because the muscles in the body use up oxygen when they move. People move their muscles a lot during exercise, meaning that they use up the oxygen in their blood more quickly. When a person does exercise, they breathe more quickly and their heart beats faster to try to get more oxygen into the body. An exercising person's heart rate can be as high as 200 beats per minute.

It's in YOUR BLOOD

Even though the heart is the most important part of the circulatory system, it would be useless without the blood. Blood carries oxygen to every single part of the body. However, this is not its only job. Blood is made up of four main things that help it to do lots of different jobs.

Red Blood Cells

Blood is made up of a lot of red blood cells. It is these red blood cells that pick up oxygen in the lungs and carry it to the rest of the body.

White Blood Cells

Blood also contains white blood cells. White blood cells help the body to stay healthy by fighting off **germs**.

Platelets

Blood also contains platelets. Platelets **repair** blood vessels when they get damaged. If you cut yourself and you didn't have any platelets in your blood, you would never stop bleeding!

Plasma

Blood is mostly made up of a substance called plasma. Plasma is a yellow liquid that contains lots of things that help the body. However, plasma's main job is to help the red blood cells, white blood cells and platelets to move through the body.

Imagine that a blood vessel is like a water slide. The water is the plasma and the people on the water slide are the red blood cells, white blood cells and platelets. The plasma helps the other things in blood to move through the blood vessels.

The plasma in blood works in the same way as the water in this slide.

This is a diagram of a drop of blood. It shows that blood is mostly made up of plasma and red blood cells.

Plasma
54%

Platelets
1%

White
blood cells
1%

Red blood
cells
44%

Over time, the different things that make up blood get used up by the body. Because of this, the body needs to keep making red blood cells, white blood cells, platelets and plasma so that it can keep making blood. Even though red blood cells, white blood cells, platelets and plasma are all important parts of blood, they are not all made in the same place.

DOWN TO THE BONE

Red blood cells, white blood cells and platelets are all made inside your bones! In the centre of bones is a soft, jelly-like substance called **bone marrow**. All of your red blood cells, all of your platelets and most of your white blood cells are made by this bone marrow.

SPILL YOUR GUTS

Plasma comes from the food and water that goes into the body. It passes into the blood from the **intestines**, which are also called the guts.

A DROP OF BLOOD

You have probably seen blood before and you might be wondering why you never saw any red blood cells or platelets in it. Well, this is because these things are so small that you can't see them without special tools.

In a drop of blood about this size there are …

… between 7,000 and 24,000 white blood cells …

… 300,000 platelets …

… and 5,000,000 red blood cells!

This is a microscope. Doctors and scientists use these to see things that are too small to see with just their eyes.

To Make a LUNG Story Short

The lungs have a very important job in the circulatory system. The lungs pull air into the body and push air out of the body. Air contains the oxygen that the body needs. This means that without the lungs, the circulatory system could not do its job.

You might think that because the body gets oxygen from the air, that the air would be mostly made up of oxygen. However, this is not true. Most of the air we breathe is made up of things that the body doesn't need.

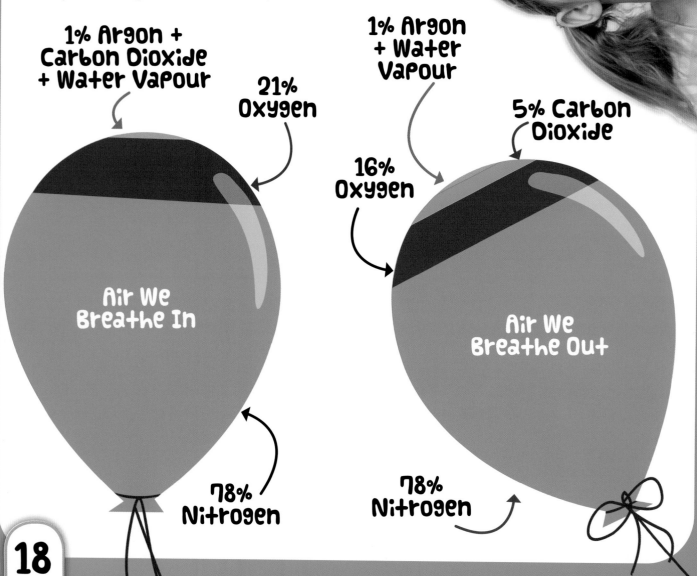

1% Argon + Carbon Dioxide + Water Vapour

21% Oxygen

1% Argon + Water Vapour

5% Carbon Dioxide

16% Oxygen

Air We Breathe In

Air We Breathe Out

78% Nitrogen

78% Nitrogen

The circulatory system takes oxygen out of the air that is in the lungs and puts it into the blood. After this, red blood cells carry the oxygen to all the muscles and organs in the body.

These red blood cells are going to the lungs to drop off carbon dioxide and pick up oxygen.

These oxygenated red blood cells are going back to the heart to be pumped around the body.

When your body uses up oxygen, it makes a gas called **carbon dioxide**. The body does not need carbon dioxide. The circulatory system takes the unwanted carbon dioxide to the lungs. The carbon dioxide in the blood is then swapped with the oxygen in the lungs. When we breathe out, we get rid of the carbon dioxide that the body doesn't need. This is why we breathe out more carbon dioxide than we breathe in!

The lungs are great at getting oxygen into the blood. They are arranged in a way that lets air spread to every corner. This makes it easier for the circulatory system to pick up oxygen. Two of the most important parts of the lungs are the bronchioles and the alveoli.

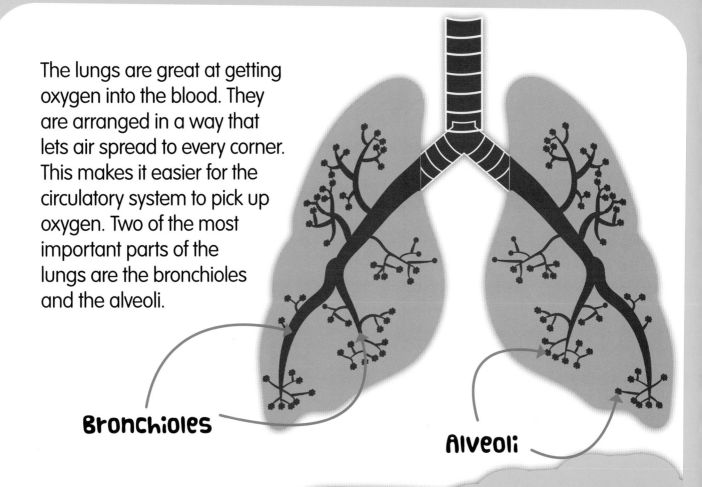

Bronchioles

Alveoli

BRONCHIOLES

Bronchioles spread through the lungs like the branches on a tree.

Bronchioles are tubes in the lungs that help to spread the air to every part of the lungs. The bronchioles start large but get smaller and smaller as they stretch further into the lungs. They also split apart like the branches on a tree. At the end of each bronchiole are very tiny sacs that fill up with air. These sacs are called alveoli.

ALVEOLI

At the end of each bronchiole are lots of very small alveoli. This is where oxygen from the lungs passes into the blood. It is also where carbon dioxide in the blood passes into the lungs so that it can be breathed out. The alveoli are covered in tiny capillaries that join up to the rest of the circulatory system.

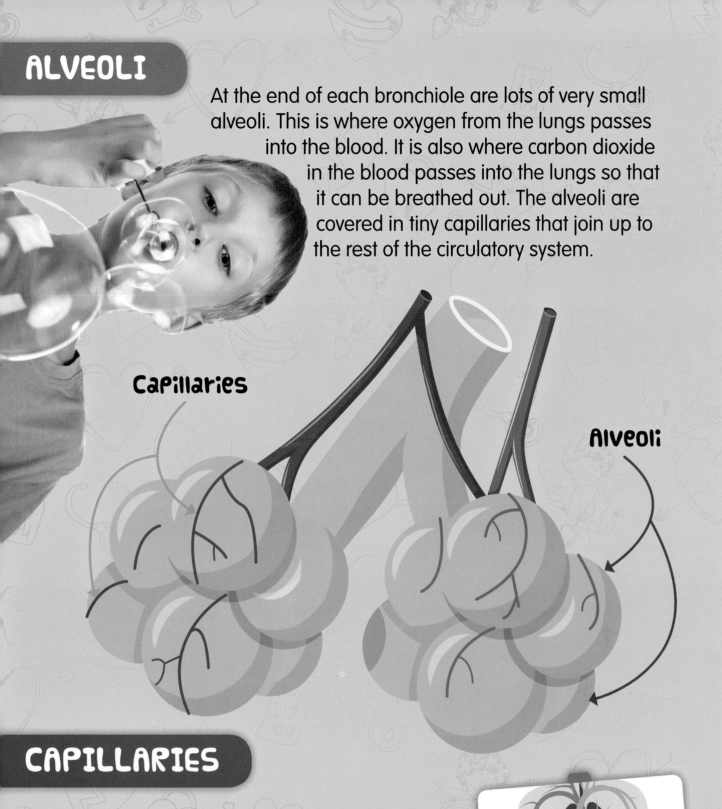

Capillaries

Alveoli

CAPILLARIES

When the bronchioles and alveoli in the lungs fill up with air, oxygen in the air can pass through the alveoli and into the capillaries. Once here, the oxygen locks onto red blood cells in the blood. At the same time, carbon dioxide in the blood can pass through the capillaries and into the alveoli. When the lungs breathe out, the carbon dioxide leaves the body.

Arteries - Why, AORTA!

All arteries take blood away from the heart. Most arteries carry oxygenated blood away from the heart and take it to the different organs and muscles in the body. However, some arteries carry deoxygenated blood away from the heart and take it to the lungs.

The biggest artery in the body is called the aorta. This is the main artery out of the heart and it takes oxygenated blood to the rest of the body. It first sends oxygenated blood to the upper body, then loops down behind the heart to send oxygenated blood to the lower body. The main artery that takes blood to the lungs is called the pulmonary artery.

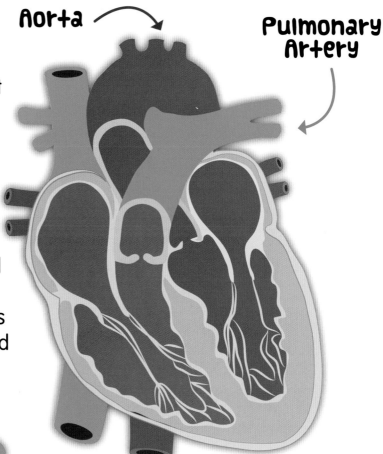

Aorta

Pulmonary Artery

Aorta

A BLUE WHALE'S AORTA is so big that a person could SWIM through it.

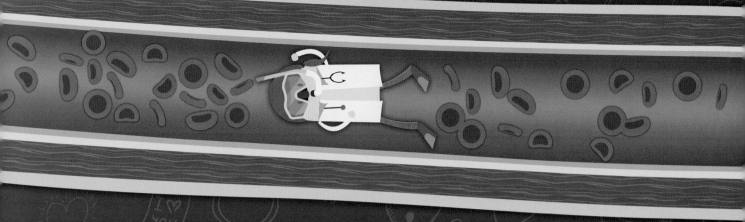

The aorta splits into smaller and smaller arteries as it gets farther away from the heart. This is because the blood needs to get to every part of the body, from the top of the head to the tips of the toes. To do this, the arteries need to split up and spread in every direction. In the end, the arteries become so small that they become capillaries.

As a tree's branches get farther away from the trunk, they get smaller. The same thing happens in the circulatory system – as the arteries get farther away from the aorta, they get smaller.

The blood in the aorta moves faster than the blood anywhere else in the body. This is because the aorta is very wide and because the blood has only just been pumped out of the heart.

BLOOD travels 40 CM through the AORTA every second.

Working in VEIN

All veins take blood towards the heart. Most veins carry deoxygenated blood from the different organs and muscles in the body back to the heart. However, some veins pick up oxygenated blood in the lungs and take it back to the heart. After this, the oxygenated blood is pumped through the aorta to the rest of the body.

Veins work in the opposite way to arteries. Veins begin when tiny capillaries start to join back together. More and more tiny veins join together, forming bigger and bigger veins. Eventually, all the veins that bring deoxygenated blood back to the heart join together to create one big vein.

Vena Cava

This upside-down tree shows how veins work. They start as tiny veins in lots of different parts of the body and then join up to make one big vein.

All of the veins in the body that carry deoxygenated blood to the heart join up to make one big vein. This vein is called the vena cava and it is the biggest vein in the entire body. All of the deoxygenated blood in the body must go through the vena cava before it can go back into the heart.

The blood in the aorta moves much more quickly than the blood in the vena cava. This is because the blood in the aorta has only just been pumped out of the heart, meaning that it is pumped with the full strength of the heart. However, the blood in the vena cava is only just about to go back into the heart after a long journey around the body, meaning that the pump from the heart is a lot weaker.

Blood in the AORTA is also helped by **gravity** as it flows **DOWNWARDS**. Blood in the VENA CAVA has to flow **UPWARDS** and fight against **GRAVITY**.

HEARTBREAKERS

Without the circulatory system, the human body could not survive. Because of this, it is very important to keep your heart as strong and healthy as possible!

Exercises such as running, swimming or cycling make the heart stronger. This is because these exercises make more blood flow to the heart than normal.

A strong heart is a happy heart!

Over time, this makes the heart bigger. It also makes the muscles in the heart stronger. Because of this, each time the heart beats it will be able to pump more blood around the body.

Exercises that make the heart stronger, such as running, swimming and cycling, are known as **cardio** exercises.

One thing that can do a lot of damage to the heart is **smoking**. Smoking also damages the blood vessels, lungs, eyes, mouth, bones and skin.

Smoking makes it more difficult for the heart to get oxygen. Like all the organs and muscles in the body, the heart needs oxygen to work properly.

When the heart doesn't get enough oxygen, it gets weaker. Over time, smoking can lead to lots of problems with the heart and the circulatory system.

Just being in the same room as someone who is **SMOKING** can **DAMAGE** your heart and lungs.

CIRCULATION
Information

1. Ancient Egyptians started to learn about the heart over 3,500 years ago.

2. Your heart beats much more slowly when you are asleep.

3. A capillary is ten times thinner than a human hair.

4. Red blood cells live for around 120 days before dying.

5. Not all blood is the same colour. Oxygenated blood is bright red, but deoxygenated blood is a lot darker.

6. A hummingbird's heart beats up to 1,250 times every minute. That's 20 times faster than a human heart!

Test in your CHEST

Use what you've just learnt to try to answer these questions. The answers are upside down at the bottom of the page.

1. Which blood vessels carry blood away from the heart?

2. What is the biggest vein in the body called?

3. What is the name for exercises that make the heart stronger?

4. In the lungs, what are at the end of bronchioles?

5. Which side of the heart takes in deoxygenated blood from the body?

6. How many times does the heart beat in one day?

7. What is the biggest artery in the body called?

8. What gas does the circulatory system take out of the body?

9. What percentage of the air we breathe is oxygen?

10. How many red blood cells are there in a drop of blood?

Answers: 1. Arteries 2. Vena Cava 3. Cardio Exercises 4. Alveoli 5. Right 6. About 100,000 7. Aorta 8. Carbon Dioxide 9. 21% 10. 5,000,000

GLOSSARY

bone marrow — the spongy tissue inside bones that makes red blood cells, white blood cells and platelets

carbon dioxide — a natural, colourless gas that is found in the air

cardio — exercises that make the heart stronger

exercise — activities that make the body more fit and healthy

gas — an air-like substance that can float around a room and often can't be seen

germs — microorganisms that cause disease

gravity — the force that pulls everything downwards, towards the centre of the Earth

hollow — has a hole or empty space in the middle

intestines — the main digestive organs, also called the gut

muscles — bundles of tissue that can contract or squeeze together

organs — parts of the body that have their own specific jobs or functions

smoking — inhaling and exhaling tobacco smoke from cigarettes

systems — sets of things that work together to do specific jobs

tissue — any material that a living thing is made out of, including humans

repair — restore something broken to a good condition

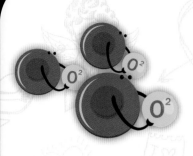

INDEX